IF ALL MEN
Are Dogs

IF ALL MEN Are Dogs

Then Women
You Hold the Leash
How Far We Go Depends on You

A Personal Account of Kevin Carr
With Contributions from Raymond Henderson

For more exclusive content visit www.ifmenaredogs.com

If All Men Are Dogs then Women You Hold the Leash: How Far We Go Depends on You
ISBN: 978-0-88144-253-3
Copyright © 2010 by Kevin Carr

Cover Designed by James Smith

CONTENTS

Preface vii

Introduction ix

Chapter 1 Men vs. Dogs 1

Chapter 2 Tighten the Chains 7

Chapter 3 Cheapskate 13

Chapter 4 Stop Letting the Dog Walk You 19

Chapter 5 Keep Out the Kennel 25

Chapter 6 Embrace the Truth 29

Chapter 7 "O What A Tangled Web We've Woven" 35

Chapter 8 Guard Your Heart 41

Chapter 9   What Do You Want From Me? .47

Chapter 10   Man Pleaser 53

Chapter 11   Never Settle! 59

Chapter 12   No Strings Attached: The New Phenomenon 63

Chapter 13   It's All About You 73

PREFACE

A former co-worker and a great friend of mine, who would not let me mention her name suggested that I write this book after one of our many conversations about men and women and the dynamics of our interactions. While sitting at her desk I began to tell her what I experienced just before coming into work that particular day. That morning I took a relative of mine to the hospital in order that her labor could be induced, so that she could have the baby that she had been carrying for the last nine months. Why me, you ask? That is the same question I asked myself. Not because I did not care for her. We practically grew up together and I would do anything for her. I just felt that such a responsibility belonged to the child's father. I asked her where he was. She told me that she had not heard from him in a few weeks. On the way to the hospital she filled me in on what had been going on in their relationship, and I came to learn that he was always in and out of her life on a consistent basis, yet still he managed to come around when he needed something. He didn't work, which meant he paid no bills. He was there and absent at the same time. Trust me there is such a thing. The only thing he contributed to their relationship was the sperm that he donated.

I now know that is a reality that many women face, but it had to hit close to home in order for me to be both affected and indicted by it at the same time. Indicted by my own often selfish nature and affected to the point where it was hard for me to understand how and why women put up with us men quite frankly. In my eyes they clearly have the power to directly influence not only the quality of their lives but also the quality of their relationships. In the midst of sharing my recent experience with my co-worker, I wondered what could be done to help. Her answer; "You should write a book." And so I did. I went back to my desk and wrote the introduction, and I have never looked back since that fateful day.

This book has been over three years in the making and it is finally here. Where my life was when I wrote the first chapter is not where I am today. In between each chapter were days and sometimes months of simply living life. Time has a way of constantly shaping and reshaping you. Some of my views have changed, some of my beliefs have faded, but one thing remains the same. My constant conviction is that women, if they would so choose to embrace it, have complete control over their lives. I do not consider myself an expert on all things related to life, love and relationships. I am not a PhD nor am I a psychiatrist. I have been a gentleman, a dog, a liar, a cheater, and a manipulator all at different segments in my life. However, the very thing that I am not, I believe makes me what I am and this is what has equipped me to present to you this book.

INTRODUCTION

LADIES... This book is dedicated to you! ALL OF YOU! Regardless of how old you are, what your race is or what your faith (religion) is, this book is for you. I have written it because I love you. I love all of you. I know some of you may be thinking, *How can you say that?* I agree those are very strong words. Trust me, when I tell you I don't use these words lightly. I'm sure most of you are thinking: *How can you love me without even knowing me---- without knowing how I look, the type of things I like, my emotions, my feelings, or my belief system?* My guess is you're wondering how I can love you without even meeting you to first determine if I like you, let alone love you. Well, ladies, believe it: it's the truth. I do love you! I love you with everything that God has placed on the inside of me. I love to see you smile. I love to see you laugh. I love it when you succeed. I love it when you pray. I love it when you're treated with respect, honor and adoration. Above all else I love it when you are treated like a WOMAN.

I love it when men (especially me) treat you like you are a part of us. I love it when we recognize how important you are, when we stop seeing just your exterior, that which is revealed to the eyes, and begin to place more value on your interior, that which can be revealed to the heart. I love it when we no longer see you only for who you are but see you for who you can be. I love when we understand your potential as a woman and the ability of that potential to impact our lives as men. I love it when we treat you how you're supposed to be treated! Some of us try. Some of us don't. Some of us won't. However, this book isn't totally about how we treat you, but rather it's about how you treat yourselves. That's what matters the most.

What if I told you that it is possible for you to never be mistreated by another man for as long as you live, Would you believe me? How does that statement make you feel? Are you curious or skeptical? It is the truth. Throughout this book we discuss the possibility of you living such a life, a life in which you are free to focus on the essential things, a life in which the majority of your problems, whether they be emotional, physical, or financial, are not caused by men. I believe all of you would love to live such a life.

Believe it or not, that's the life you should be living. Things are hard enough. The mortgage needs to be paid. The lights need to stay on and the cable bill is due. Life is too precious and way too short to spend the majority of your time fretting over a man. Before you read any further I want to ask you to please do me a favor. Take a few minutes to evaluate your life. Evaluate how the man in your life has been treating you, whether it is a husband, friend, or boyfriend. Once you've done this, begin to think about how you would like to be treated, how you feel you should be treated, and most importantly how you believe God created you to be treated. As you do this, it is important that you are honest with yourself. If you get in the habit of believing your own lies, you will surely become accustomed to believing the lies of other people. (This possibly could have been how it all started.) Once you've completed this, continue to read on, but keep those thoughts in the back of your mind as you go throughout the book. If you keep an open mind and an open heart as you read these pages, I hope to begin the process of helping to change your life. It's not what's written on these pages but rather what you allow yourself to take from them that has the ability to cause your life to never be the same again. Let the first chapter be a fresh start. Let it be the doorway to life at another level. Let it be the beginning of change. Let it alter how you see your life, how you see the men around you, and most importantly how you see yourself.

Chapter *1*

MEN VS. DOGS

I've always heard women say things like "all men are dogs" or "he ain't nothing but a no-good dog." I never paid much attention to these statements until recently when I decided to write this book. As I began my preparations I became intrigued about what these statements really meant. I wondered how two distinctly different species could have anything in common with one another. I questioned several women to see what I could uncover. I began to ask women how men and dogs relate in their eyes.

First, I asked several women, "Have you ever called a man a dog?" Nine out of ten women answered "yes." Intrigued, I asked them why. Most of the women I asked answered, "Because men only care about what they can get out of a relationship." Most of these women felt that this factor was sex. One woman said that all men want to do is hump you and move on to the next woman and do the same. Most of the ladies with whom I talked seem to be tired of these types of men running in and out of their lives. They are tired of the games. They crave something that is concrete as well as fulfilling. They want substance! They want something of value, and even more so, they want something that adds value to their lives as women.

Frustration has set in because what they have been looking for they have yet to find, and what they expect they have yet to receive. Sometimes after not getting what we believe we should have over a long period of time (as people) we have the tendency to adopt the belief that it isn't available. **Thus, many women have come to believe all men are dogs**. This definitely seems to be a hasty generalization that can be argued. Sometimes the truth isn't always the truth. Sometimes it's just the easiest thing to believe at the moment. Are all men dogs? I find it hard to believe that they are. Are some men dogs? Maybe so. Let's find out!

Let's look at some characteristics of dogs and see if we can relate any of them to men in one way or another. Dogs live by instinct. Like all animals, instinct controls everything they do. They live solely off impulse and feeling. It may be safe to say, unlike humans, a dog doesn't have emotions or a conscience to govern its actions. Instinct is to a dog as a program is to a computer. It is easy to assume dogs live according to that program. It is almost impossible for them to deviate outside of what they've been programmed to do. Honestly, many of us men operate in this same manner. We talk, act, and think in many cases the way we have been programmed. We are constantly influenced by our fathers or lack thereof, friends, and other environmental factors. That doesn't give us men a free pass, because unlike humans, dogs do not have free will or the gift of choice. You can train a dog but you can never change a dog. A dog is what it is. It can never be anything else. You never have to worry about your pit bull acting like your cat. It will never happen. Let us now re-focus on men.

Let's explore the concept of men being dogs and discover if there is any validity to that statement. Ladies, this may be hard for you to believe, but men are not dogs. It's genetically impossible! However, I admit that at times we men have some doglike tendencies. For instance, most dogs are very aggressive. So are most men. Dogs can't always convey their emotions in a way where they are easily understandable, which could lead to the belief that they aren't present. A lot of men suppress their emotions to the point it seems they don't have any either. In my personal life the biggest complaint that I have received from women has been that my unwillingness to invest my emotions into a relationship often leaves them to play the guessing game regarding my true feelings. I've had a woman remark that I seem like a shell, as in I'm physically present, but absent are my emotions which contain my inner most thoughts and feelings. Many times we men put up walls, juggle several women at a time and run from commitment, all in an attempt to cover our own insecurities. Dogs are physical. They sniff, lick, and do a whole list of other interesting things. So do men. Many would agree that this is how we were created. With many women, intimacy can begin with a deep conversation. By opening up, one begins to give of oneself to another person. Unlike women, for many men, intimacy doesn't start until sexual intercourse.

There were moments in my life when I wasn't the least bit interested in a woman's conversation. I couldn't have cared less about her innermost thoughts and feelings. I couldn't connect with them even if I tried. My emotions were suppressed to the point where they were inactive, and to be quite frank, I didn't mind it at all. My priority was what I could get from a woman---- namely intercourse. In my mind intercourse was the pinnacle of intimacy. I was wrong. Contrary to popular belief, intercourse is not the most powerful form of intimacy. In fact, it is only one form of it. When one reaches a place where one is able to open up oneself, it allows someone to see him/her for who he/she really is. When one allows one's most intricate parts to be seen, which encompass all sides of that person, that's intimacy. In many relationships men skip this part and head straight for intercourse, i.e.. my personal example above. Because of this, many relationships suffer and lots of women are left unfulfilled even if they've been physically satisfied for the moment. That's all it is, a moment. To enjoy the moment is good, but it is better to use each moment we have wisely so that we may enjoy a lifetime.

Many relationships are suffering as a result of selfishness. Did I mention dogs are selfish by nature? If someone ever wanted to test that statement, all he would have to do is take his dog out for a walk in the park on a sunny afternoon. Think about when a dog wants to eat: it rummages through the garbage; when it has to go to the bathroom it scratches on the door; when it sees a cat it pursues it at all costs; and when it's horny, well I think we all know what happens then. Specifically with male dogs, it is how they were created. It often seems as if dogs act without thinking first.

Unfortunately many men act in this same manner. Life revolves around them. As a result everything around them, specifically women, suffers. Selfishness kills relationships! It kills marriages and it causes people to get hurt. I believe the number one component to a successful relationship is a commandment given by Jesus: Love your neighbor as you love yourself (Mark 12:31).

If you are in a relationship, just imagine what it would be like if you lived by that. I guarantee if more of us would apply this principle to our lives we would have a lot fewer divorces, and even more marriages. I guess it makes sense that they call a dog *man's best friend*. We do have some similarities in our actions and tendencies. I would say the number one thing men and dogs have in common is selfishness. In essence it is common for them to think more about themselves than those around them.

In many cases we don't think about how our actions affect those around us. For me to cheat is an act of selfishness. For me to think more about my wants and needs than those of my woman is an act of selfishness. Selfishness is embedded in human nature. It is our ability to subdue and control it that will determine not only the quality of our relationships but also the quality of our lives. When a man goes from one woman to the next, when he cheats, when he pursues only physical pleasure from women, he is living based on instinct. In these cases instinct has infected character. This isn't an excuse; it's the truth!

However that is not how GOD intends for men to live. He did not make us to live like animals (not being able to control our desires). The lives of men are supposed to revolve around responsibility and purpose. So *you* don't have to and *you* shouldn't settle for this type of behavior from men. I just want you to understand why we do the things we do. I say we because I'm a man and deal with the same things, but every day I make a conscious effort to put others before myself.

Some days I am successful. Some days I'm not. My goal is to live a selfless lifestyle. I recently asked myself a question. I asked myself how long I would keep taking from women with whom I come into a relationship. I questioned myself about when I am going to care more about them than my own selfish desires. I challenged myself to begin to treat women how I would want my mother, daughter or little sister to be treated by a man. So again, I apologize for the way we have been treating you. I personally apologize to every woman I have disrespected, to every woman from whom I've ever taken anything. I APOLOGIZE. If you are reading this book, I need you to understand, even though you may have been mistreated in the past, or if you're even being mistreated currently, you don't have to be! It is your choice; you have more power than you recognize. Are some men dogs? Yes. However, it's your choice what type of man you attach yourself to. You don't have to turn your life into an animal shelter. In case you weren't aware of it, there are men who are just that. They are men in all aspects of the word. Then, there are some who have yet to walk in true manhood. Ladies, take your pick. But please remember to not complain about what **you** have picked for yourself.

TIGHTEN THE CHAINS

L adies, respect yourselves enough not to allow yourselves to be disrespected --- especially on a continual basis. I do not doubt that you will come across disrespectful people (that's a given), but it is your choice whether or not you allow them to be part of your life. We determine whom we allow to get close to us. Even once we grant a person access to our lives, we have the ultimate authority either to continue to grant them that access or to revoke it. Have you ever seen someone walking a dog with the type of leash that can be made tighter around the dog's neck? This is to keep the dog in check. In most cases it is very effective. I can remember walking my dog Bandit when I was younger and thinking to myself, *This is great.* I marveled at the fact that I was able to control a dog that was twice as strong as I was. Every time the dog tried to cross the line and do something I didn't want him to do, I would just pull the leash a little tighter around the neck, and he would get the picture and eventually calm down and submit. He soon realized that I was in control. Some of you reading this book should apply this to your personal lives. You should set boundaries in your life and you shouldn't permit anyone to cross them without your consent. Don't allow men to talk to you any kind of way. Don't permit them to approach you any kind of way. Stop turning around when one of us whistles at you. If you get approached disrespectfully by a man, that can be a sign of what you will be dealing with from that particular person on an ongoing basis.

The way a man approaches you can often determine how he views you, which will likewise influence the way he will treat you. Men are observers: we are able to see the image you give off as a woman. By this I mean many times we are able to spot the insecure, the bitter, and even the shallow, and we approach each one according to the image we see. The solution is to take control of your lives! Take control of your mind and your emotions! One way to take control is by making sure the image that you have of yourself is a positive one. We can't control the lives of others even though some of us try, but we can control our own lives. Decide to become responsible for you! Become responsible for your own happiness, your own fulfillment, and your own satisfaction. When you learn to depend on yourself for these things, the actions of others will have a minimal effect on you. Don't give men all of your power. It is my observation that most women depend on men too much. Let me clarify. I don't find anything wrong with women depending on men for certain things. Not at all. However, I do have an issue with women who depend on men for their livelihood.

A lot of women are unhappy and unfulfilled because they are depending on men to make them happy and to fulfill their needs. If you are one of those women, you will be waiting forever. The fact is, it will never happen. As a man it's not my job to make you happy and fulfilled. (I couldn't do it even if I tried.) Yes, I can contribute to your happiness, but I am certainly not the source of it. When you learn to depend on yourself for those things, you will see that no person can complete your happiness and fulfill all of your needs.

The bottom line is this: if you are unhappy and unsatisfied as a single woman, you will continue to be that way even in a relationship with a man. What some women don't understand is that men are just a portion of the puzzle but not the puzzle itself. One piece doesn't make the puzzle what it is, even though it may add to it or even complete it. Have you ever met someone with an inconsistent personality? One day they're happy, the next they're sad. One day they're motivated, the next they're not. To bring it more into perspective, one week they're through with their man, the next they're back to being madly in love again. For many, their mood, their demeanor, even their outlook on life seems to change like the weather. Many people live this way. Since this book is focused on the female persuasion, let's discuss the effects such a lifestyle can have on you. First of all, women who live like this are very unstable. They're constantly going up and down like a roller coaster.

The truth is, that's the nature of life. It's up and down. Life is constantly changing. It's never the same. It evolves from one day to the next. Imagine if you lived in South Florida and your emotions, your attitude, and even your perspective on life were based on the weather forecast for that day. One would be all over the place. Let's just say when it rained one would be sad; when there was lightning one would be confused; and when it was sunny one would be happy. Now just think about that for a moment. Imagine how hectic one's life would be if this were true. If any of you have ever frequented Florida you have an idea of how unpredictable the weather can be at times. It could be sunny; then all of a sudden it will rain like cats and dogs only to become sunny again, then rain once more two hours later. This could also be followed by a lightning storm brought on by an approaching cold front. Wow! Sounds hectic.

If one's emotions were tied to that, it would be draining, in all aspects of the word, emotionally, physically, and mentally. This may be a surprise to you, but many women are presently living this way. For many the stability of their emotions is contingent on the stability of their relationships. As the relationship goes, so goes their emotions. Instead of their emotions being tied to the weather they are tied to a man. This can be a dangerous place to be. At this place what he does ultimately determines what you do. This should not be. Now this isn't to say that you shouldn't attach yourself emotionally to a man, nor is it meant to deter you from being emotionally intimate with a man, or opening up your heart to him. That in itself can be a beautiful thing. However, that doesn't mean he ought to control the stability of your emotions. That's your responsibility. After all, they are your emotions. Many say things like "I can't help how I feel." This may be true, but you can decide who you have feelings for. I can't help that if I put my hands in fire I'm going to feel burned. That's a given. But I can help by not putting my hands in the fire in the first place.

As a single man who has come across my fair share of women, it has been my observation that many women don't have enough standards. I can remember thinking at times, *Man, that was too easy,* when it came to some of my dealings with women. We'll discuss this more in later chapters, but it's the truth.

Let's once again look at our new best friend, Bandit. When you first get a puppy, it would be unwise to just go to the park, unhook the leash, and expect it to behave. Those owners seen walking side by side with their unleashed dogs are those who have gained their dog's honor and respect. They did so by setting boundaries, which in turn set the outline of how their dog should behave. More women should do this with their men. Sometimes I wonder why so many women insist on letting men treat their hearts like a park and like untrained puppies they run all over doing their business wherever they please with no regard for their actions. This is one of the most important chapters in this book. It is important to understand that you have the ability to determine the quality of your life, along with the quality of your relationships. It is that ability that must be exercised if you are to ever experience what you truly desire.

We've already determined that you can't control the actions of others, but we've also determined that you can control the effects you allow such actions to have on you. You can't control if your man cheats on you. You could try your best to make sure you've found the right man, but even then it comes down to his morals and values along with his love and respect for you. I've talked to women who constantly complain about the actions of their men. They continually grumble about their man's selfish nature. They cry day after day about being hurt and heart-broken. Every time I have encountered such women I've managed to hold my tongue. More than a few times it took everything in me not to tell these women the truth. Honestly, I'm probably at fault for not doing so. The truth is, the problems these women are facing, the heartache, the pain, and the drama engulfing their lives, are not being caused by the men they are blaming. To the shock of most, those problems are being caused by the person right under their noses. Themselves. They're at the root of their own problems. It's much easier to label others as responsible for what is wrong in our own lives instead of just taking responsibility and correcting what needs to be fixed. Let me just say this as plainly as possible. If your boyfriend or husband is unfaithful to you on a continual basis and you know about it, it's your fault. Period. So don't shed another tear, don't argue anymore, do not utter another complaint, because until you DECIDE that you will not tolerate it anymore, the blame lies with you and you alone. If a man knows he can do things of that nature and still have you by his side, he has no motivation to stop. Better yet he has no incentive to change. There's a big difference between stopping and changing. Stopping is merely temporary.

I've stopped doing lots of things only to start doing them again. It wasn't until I changed in specific areas that I was able to break those bad habits. Change is permanent. Once a caterpillar changes into a butterfly it never goes back to its former state. When people change, their actions change. The bottom line is this: men can only go as far as you let them. So if your man has crossed the boundaries that you have set, if he has been going about his business with little regard for your relationship, tighten the leash. Are you walking the dog or is the dog walking you? Remember, you must be honest with yourself; it is the only way you will ever change.

Before you turn another page, before you attempt to read another chapter, you must first DECIDE at this very moment to become responsible. You must DECIDE that you will not tolerate being treated like a whore any longer. DECIDE you will not allow yourself to be beat upon anymore. DECIDE you will not be manipulated again. Finally, DECIDE that you don't need a man to help you be who you already are. If you have made those life-changing decisions, you may continue reading. If you haven't made those decisions, you might as well give this book to someone else, because the rest of it is not for you.

CHEAPSKATE

You know something? Life is funny. I know plenty of women who spend countless dollars on themselves. They spend money on things such as manicures, pedicures, facials, makeup, and high-priced clothes. Ironically, these are some of the cheapest women I know. You see, they are willing to pay whatever cost for the minute things in life, all the while expecting the thing that matters the most to be given to them for free. The thing that most women aren't willing to pay for is what the magnificent Aretha Franklin spelled out in her hit song "RESPECT". Very few women receive respect because very few of them are willing to pay for it. Respect is not given until you first earn it or essentially pay for it. Those who expect it to be given to them free of charge are those who never receive it. Everybody should want respect but not everyone receives it.

People always suggest different keys to having successful relationships. Some say commitment is key; others say honesty is vital, which may be true. One of the most important keys often forgotten is respect. Respect means to care for, to honor, and to esteem. When two people have little or no respect for one another, they treat each other any kind of way. As a result, their relationship suffers. Let's look at an example of this to which most of us can relate. If an employer doesn't have the respect of his employees, the quality of his business will soon deteriorate. Employees will come and go as they please. They'll come late, take extra long lunch breaks, and work in a lackadaisical manner. There is no respect in this relationship; therefore both parties will never be satisfied. Can any of you relate this behavior to your man's? Does he act with little or no regard for your feelings, wants, and needs? Does he honor you? Does he esteem you? If not, he doesn't respect you. If your man doesn't respect you, it's not his fault, it's yours. It is your fault! If you must ask for respect, you don't deserve it and you will never get it. <u>Your life and all that comes with it is your responsibility</u>! What GOD does is put the clay in your hands; you must shape, mold, scope, and process how you want your life to be. You were born to be a visionary: therefore if you can't see it, it cannot be.

Before starting this book I surveyed several women about how they felt a man they were involved with should treat them. They said various things. Some said like a queen: others said with love and others said with loyalty. I asked all types of women: white, black, young, and old and women from many different walks of life. They all have so little yet so much in common. Even though each woman had a different answer for that question, each of them said she wanted to be treated with respect. Even more interesting was that the majority of the women I surveyed had been in previous relationships in which they were disrespected on a continual basis. The majority of the women who said they wanted their man to treat them with respect were never treated that way at all. So that's proof that wanting a thing doesn't guarantee that you'll get it. Now that we understand that respect isn't free, let's discover what we have to do to get it.

Some women want men to "like" them more than they want them to respect them. In fact many confuse the two (mistaking one for the other when they are completely different). Just because a man "likes" you doesn't mean that he respects you. In my life, most of the women I respected were the ones I did not "like." It's not that I disliked them as people, but rather I didn't find those women agreeable with my agenda.

My motives were self- centered, to say the least. Many times in my interactions with women I wasn't looking for a "meaningful" relationship; I was looking for someone to use to help fulfill my needs. So in turn if you had to label my affection for those women, they were the ones that I didn't "like." However, they were the ones I respected. You see, the women who fit my agenda, the ones I "liked," the women to whom I could say and do what I wanted, the ones who gave me themselves with me having to expend little to no effort, these were the ones that I "liked." Even though I "liked" them, I didn't respect them at all. They didn't earn my respect so they were disrespected. These women were more worried about receiving my affection than receiving my respect. This consequently caused them to receive neither.

How can a man value you as a woman if you don't first place value on your own self? As people we have the tendency to neglect things when they come to us too easily. If playing *hard to get* is what it will take for you to get a little respect, then by all means I suggest you do it. A guy may not like the fact that he can't get "any" on the first date. He may not like that he can't have it at all. He might be offended by the standards you've set in your life. That's the price you pay for respect. There have been quite a few times while dropping a woman off at her house after a good time at dinner I assumed and expected sex to be the next item on the menu, only for it to be made very clear to me that it was not going to be quite that easy. Often times I left the presence of these women with a higher regard for them. To get respect, sometimes you have to do what is not popular. He may talk about you to your face, but I guarantee that he will respect you behind your back. Yes, you read right. He may call you names, but as he walks away he will have a newfound respect for you even if he doesn't show it to your face. I can personally attest to this.

I was talking to one of my cousins about this very subject. He was telling me about a young lady whom he had met a few days before. He was telling me that after only a few days of knowing each other she had sex with him. He then told me that he wasn't going to call her again. When I asked why, he responded, "For what?" He then began to talk about his ex-girlfriend. The moment he brought her up you could tell the difference between how he viewed the two women. He said, "Man, she made me wait six months!" What he really was implying was that she made him respect her. Please understand the actions of my cousin were no better than those of the particular woman. However, in regards to the theme of this book his actions are irrelevant. I use this example to help you get into the minds of men. It is my hope that if I illustrate how men think about certain things, you will be influenced in a positive way. Then maybe, just maybe, you will begin to think about these things before you decide to take any further particular course of action regarding your relationships.

Another aspect of Respect is difficult to gain, and easy to lose. Many times in life it is harder to get something back after you've given it away. Think about the people that you have come across during your life thus far. Can you recall any instances that caused you to lose a certain amount of respect for a person? Once that level of respect is gone you look at them differently. Because you view them differently you treat them differently. One treats a person how he/she sees that person. The same can be said for men and women.

We men treat women based on how we see them, and how we see you as women can often be based on how you see yourself. The image that you give off is most likely the same image folks understand to be the true YOU. If you pay attention to people as you interact with them you can get a sense of how they feel about themselves. One can tell the confident from the arrogant. One can distinguish between a person who is humble and a person who just has low self-esteem.

Another thing that dogs and men have in common is that they both are observant. If you see a scary looking dog and he growls, the moment you become afraid he can sense it. Your reaction to his action determines what he does next. The same goes for men. While interacting with you, some men are able to pick up the little things that make you who you are, and he in turn acts accordingly. Men with selfish motives tend to only get into relationships with those women who complement their agenda. A man with doglike tendencies will exploit your shortcomings as a woman to get what he wants. Dog-like men prey on women with low self-confidence. These women have yet to figure out who they really are. Once this type of man becomes aware that you are depending on him to define who you are, he will surely take advantage of it. Some of you may be thinking that's a little too deep, but in all actuality it isn't. Just think about it.

This is why some older men pursue younger girls. It's not about age; it is about control. These types of men seek younger ladies because a lot of times these are the ones who have yet to come into their own. Mentally they have not yet come to a full realization of who they are. A lot of men use this to their advantage by shaping such women into what they want them to be. You can learn a lot about a man by making note of the type of women he pursues on a consistent basis. Most insecure men don't like to be involved with confident women. They feel threatened by them. Men who are very controlling seek women who allow themselves to be controlled.

Let's finish up with this topic of respect. The bottom line comes down to whether you are willing to pay for it or not. For each of you the cost may be different. Some of you may have to do without a man for a while. Isn't that better than having to settle for just anyone? Some may have to do without sex. Isn't that better than being treated like a piece of meat? How much is respect worth to you? That will determine how much you are willing to pay for it. When a man respects you, you'll know it. It is not your mission in life to get men to respect you. It is your duty to respect yourself, to honor, esteem, value, and uplift your own self. How can anybody ever know that you are valuable if you don't?

Chapter 4

STOP LETTING
THE DOG WALK YOU

Imagine this. You are out for a jog in the park and all of a sudden you notice something extremely strange. You look a second time to be certain that what you're seeing is really happening: you pinch yourself to be sure that you're not dreaming. You can't believe your eyes. What you are seeing seems so unreal and outright ridiculous. You begin to ask yourself *how something like this could have transpired*. You have seen plenty of people walk dogs before, but for as long as you have walked God's green earth you have never seen a dog walking a human being. *It's crazy*, you think to yourself. *How could a person let such a thing happen?* You're wondering why someone would go along with this and allow themselves to be treated in such a manner with what seems to be no sense of concern at all. Oddly enough, while you are amazed and confused the person in question thinks this behavior is perfectly normal.

You are outraged that a fellow human being is being treated in such a shameful fashion. You question, *Why don't they just put a stop to this?* One may think, *If only they knew the power they have.* This is a sad situation to witness.

Here is a human being openly degraded when they don't have to be. Even though one may think this is about as far from reality as one ever gets, this is a reality for many of you reading this book. A lot of women don't recognize how much power they really have. I need you to understand what I mean by this. In this situation the word power means CONTROL more than anything else. Some try to use the superficial to try to gain control over a situation. Many think that sex gives them power over men when it doesn't at all. Sure, your body may get you through some doors in life, but even on the other side of those doors you will still be *power-less*. Every time you compromise who you are to gain something out of life, you become less powerful as a person. Instead of controlling a situation, you are the one being controlled. Instead of paying the price to get where they want to be in life, these women settle and become subject to the conditions set forth by others. Instead of walking the dog, they are the ones being taken out for the walk.

Let me pose to you this question: If you can't be you then who can you be? For many the hardest thing to do in life is to be themselves. Their biggest challenge is to be able to conduct their lives the way they see fit and to allow their true thoughts and feelings to be seen through their actions. For example, let's take a look into the music industry. We'll create our own singing sensation and use her to illustrate our point. Let's name her Peaches. She is a new artist who is extremely talented, is drop-dead gorgeous, and can flat-out sing. But our Peaches faces a dilemma. She has always based her music on the way she leads her life, consistent with her moral values. Unfortunately the people at the record label don't think this type of music will sell records. They tell her she must go with what sells. Reluctantly, she agrees and goes against her moral values and follows the advice of those around her. By the time her first single comes out she is a completely different artist. Because "sex" sells, she wears next to nothing in her video shoots and during her performances. She always believed that sex was for marriage, but now most of her songs are about steamy one-night stands.

When the album is finally released it's a huge hit. It flies off the shelf in just a few weeks. She is a success, right? Wrong! She is not successful at all. The person she is pretending to be is. In her case, to accomplish her goals she lost herself.

If you have to become someone else to get to a particular place in life, you probably don't belong there. Some of you may think I'm splitting hairs on this topic, but once again I ask if you can't be yourself, then who can you be? Live life; don't let life live you. I was once acquainted with a female who brought this subject to light. We started going out regularly, and as time passed we became attracted to each other (well, at least I was attracted to her). One day we had a conversation about where things were headed between us. During the conversation she began to explain to me that she wasn't looking for a relationship at this point in her life. Of course being a man I shoved this aside as mere silly talk and assumed that once she got to know me more, she wouldn't be able to help herself. My ego assured me that my boyish charm would win her over! Weeks passed and nothing changed. By this time, I was completely confused. I couldn't comprehend what could possibly be wrong with her (or me). After all, I thought that I was the best thing from "Philly" since cheese steaks, but she was not budging. It wasn't until I began writing this chapter that I finally recognized what was going on.

She was walking the dog and not letting it walk her. At an age in which most young women are involved with at least one man, she managed not to conform and stay focused on what she wanted out of life. She was able to overcome her feelings (which is very important). She also overcame the opinions of others and the pressures of life. She was able to be who she wanted to be despite who others thought she should be. You will never be comfortable in life until you are able to be yourself. Take inventory of those in your life around whom you are most comfortable. Those are the people whom you let see the real you.

We'll discuss more of this later. But for now back to the matter at hand. I've always wondered why so many women let men get away with so much. At times I feel like some women make things too easy for men. They let us talk to them with no reverence. They permit us to sleep with them without knowing our true characters. They make us more important than we really are. PLEASE remember this is coming from a man!

As a result, it has also been my observation that many women are too "needy." What I mean is that they feel like they *need* a man. Do you as a woman need a man? Of course! The truth is we need each other. As a man I need you just as much as you need me. We can't create a child without each other. We can't successfully raise one to its full potential without each other. We can't become truly complete without each other. That's the purpose of marriage, for two to become one and thus complete each other.

Some don't recognize this, but it's important as a woman for you to gain a sense of your own self worth. This is imperative. If you don't first think that you are worthy of a certain thing, you will not have the fortitude to expect it, let alone the ability to require it. What do you require? Will you take just any man? Or do you require a faithful one? Does he have to be devoted to only you, or is being his "side dish" okay with you? Do you require him to have a job? I asked these questions because what you require is a clear picture of what you think you are worthy of. You are worth much more than you can ever imagine. You are God's own handiwork. Have you ever been in a situation in which you **really** needed something? A lot of times you were willing to do certain things that you normally wouldn't do to have that particular thing in your life. The same is true for women and men. Some women think they need men more than they really do. Because of this they'll do certain things or put up with certain things to either get a man or keep him around. They're not walking the dog; the dog is walking them.

You see, the topic of this book is men, but the theme of it is you. I know I said it before but I want to reiterate: a man can only go as far as you let him. You essentially hold the leash. You just have to realize it. If you don't want to have sex, then don't. If you don't want to be in a relationship, don't be. If you want a man to be faithful and committed to you, don't settle for anything less. This is where self-worth comes into play the most. It is when you are at the place of decision-making. The greater the value that you place on yourself, the greater your capacity will be to make better decisions that will ultimately uplift your life. It's not that we don't want what's better for our lives. I'm positive that most of us do. However, it is our ability to do better that will determine if we will ever have better. Walk the dog, don't let it walk you.

You *need* a man but you don't *need* a man. If a man ever tells you that he doesn't need you, he is lying. He may be thinking he doesn't need you because he has somewhere else to go but who cares; let him leave. As a matter of fact, some of you need to do just that. Let him leave! Why are you holding on? He doesn't treat you right anyway. You don't need him. Some of you have men who don't want to leave because you've allowed them to develop a comfort zone in terms of your relationship. You refuse to challenge their behavior and you continue to allow them to do what they want when they want. You need to let go and let them leave. Some of your lives are sinking because you insist on holding on to the anchor. It's time for you to grab the steering wheel of your life and turn it in the direction that you want to go.

KEEP OUT THE KENNEL

One reason a lot of women can't find a good man could be because they have yet to find themselves. Many times you have to identify who you are as a person and come to grips with the direction you want your life to go before you include somebody else in the equation. If you are clueless about who you are and where you're going, it's impossible for you to truly recognize what kind of man fits your life the best. You wouldn't really know what to look for. You will take anything in hopes that it turns out to be the right thing. Sometimes you just need some alone time. Growing up, most of my brothers and sisters didn't live with me. I had lots of alone time. Of course I had lots of friends, but once I was in the house it was just me. As a kid I would get bored, but as I grew older I began to value this alone time. Now I love to spend a day or so around the house by myself. It quiets things down for me. It allows me to concentrate and focus on my life and the direction it's heading. It is during these times that I often ask myself, *What is it that I want out of life?.* What do you want out of life, ladies? What are some of your dreams, goals, and aspirations? If you don't have dreams, what's the use of waking up in the morning? I once read a statement in a book written by Edwin Louis Cole and I will never forget it. It read, "The two greatest days of a [person's] life are the day they are born and the day they find out why they were born."

Once you get a sense of purpose, your life will change. It will affect the things you do and the people with whom you are involved. It will change everything! This too relates to your dealings with men. You should only become involved with men who can help you.

Please don't mistake that for being selfish. There are two types of people in your life: those who help you and those who hurt you. There is no middle ground. It's your job to recognize both and act accordingly. Let's look at a practical example.

If you dreamed of one day becoming president of the United States (which we now know is possible), knowing the type of research they do on your background, why would you ever involve yourself with a drug dealer? Can you see how that could hinder your dream? Once you find out who you are and where you're going, it will impact the type of men you allow in your life. Let me clarify something because I don't want anyone to take this the wrong way. I'm not suggesting that you find a man who seems like he can help you accomplish your dreams physically. Not at all. Your dreams are your responsibility. So if you're an aspiring singer you don't have to be romantically involved with the CEO of a record company to be successful in the music business. You might just need a man who is supportive of you, one who is there when you need him.

Lots of women go from man to man and never find what they're looking for. Instead they wind up in one bad relationship after another. If you keep running into the wrong men, it may help if you take your eyes off them and focus on you.

It is important to focus on you because YOU are the most important person in your life. The state of your being determines the state of your life. Knowing where you are presently is vital. If you have ever tried to read a road map, you know it can be confusing at times. You see all types of streets and objects. After a few minutes it can begin to look like a poorly put together crossword puzzle. When reading a map most people try to find the place they are trying to reach first and then devise a plan how to get there. It may seem logical but it hardly ever works. And when it does it causes unneeded stress. When reading a map you must first identify where you are presently. Your destination then becomes a lot clearer, not to mention easier to reach. Find yourself before you find a man (read that again). I don't know if you are aware of this, but you weren't put on earth to just cook, clean, raise children, and at times re-raise your man. If you're a businesswoman, you weren't born to just work a nine- to- five job, nowadays eight- to -six. You are here on purpose, for a purpose.

God made all of us for a specific reason. You must find out what that reason is. A lot of people don't like being single because they are looking at it the wrong way. They look at time alone as time being spent by themselves rather than time being *spent on themselves*. On whom are you spending your time? Is he worth it? If time were money, some of you would have given away your life savings. I ask again, is he really worth the time you're spending on him? If so, *great!* If not, recognize it and understand that unlike money the time you spend you'll never see again. Lots of you invest so much in relationships and so little in yourselves. The most valuable asset you will ever have in life is yourself. With that said, where in the world can you find a "good man"? Is it church? How about at the work- place? What about college? It all depends on who you are and what you're looking for. From what I hear, a "good man" is hard to find. That doesn't mean there aren't any good men. It could just be you're having trouble rec-ognizing them.

In my own experiences I believe lots of women run into good men, but it seems they don't know what to do when they meet them. Some-times I think some women become used to being treated like second-class citizens and they become immune to it. Then when someone comes around to treat them differently, they push that person away. That's the reason you have to stay out of the kennel for a while and spend some time on yourself. It's okay to be single and to take some time to work on YOU. That way you can pinpoint the difference between a dog and a man. Every man isn't a dog. You have to learn to see the difference. My advice to you: find out who you are, where you are, and where you want to go, and then build your life around that. Once you do this your life takes on a genuine sense of purpose. It is said there are three types of people: those who make things happen, those who watch things happen, and those who ask what happened. Which one are you? This coincides with our earlier discussion about re-taking control of your life. Spend some time on yourself. It will be the greatest investment that you will ever make.

Chapter 6

EMBRACE THE TRUTH

The truth hurts! Man, ain't that the truth (no pun intended). The reality is that the truth hurts so much that a lot of us hide it from ourselves. It's hard to face the reality of what's really going on in our lives. Often it's much easier to just convince ourselves that everything is fine. Be honest with yourself. Things will never change until you change them. In many instances it isn't that your man is lying to you but more like you are lying to yourself. That's why you feel the way you feel. Why do you continue to make excuses for your man's behavior? Whom are you really trying to convince? Sometimes we believe things not because they're true but because it's more comfortable for us to deal with. For some women it's easier to believe that they have a "good man," one who is faithful and committed to them, than to deal with the fact that they are with a "dog." In our lives, sometimes the thing that is hardest for us to see seems obvious to everyone else. We must learn to take things for exactly what they are and act accordingly.

Call a spade a spade. Over time I have come to learn that women have a very strong sense of intuition. Trust it, ladies. There have been numerous times when I have been accused of cheating, flirting, and a host of other things. All those things I was guilty of at one time or another, but because I was able to hold my ground at denying the allegations, the dust would eventually settle and I would be back in good graces in the relationship soon enough.

Character is what makes a man. It's what defines him. So when you're judging a man do so by his character. Stop listening to what men say and start watching what they do. You know the old saying: *Actions speak louder than words.* It's the truth. Until you own up to this reality your life will never change. I know it's not easy to do. In fact, this may be one of the hardest things you will ever have to do in life. But it's worth it. It's easy for me to look at your life and make assessments based on what I see. It's easy for me to tell you what you should be doing; that's not hard at all. But it's up to you. If you only get one thing from this book, please come to grips with the fact that it's up to you. It's your choice. Choice is one of the greatest gifts that God has given us.

Your choices make your life what it is, and they will also determine where it will be in the future. Some choices are easy and some are hard, but they all influence our lives either for the good or for the bad. If you want to know the truth about your life, just *ask* yourself. You can lie to yourself, but your self will never lie to you. Listen to your heart. In life when we aren't where we are supposed to be, our hearts tend to let us know. Some of us block it out better than others; nevertheless it's still there. Just listen to it. Have you ever done something that even though you could come up with plenty of things to support what you were doing, somewhere deep down in your heart you knew it wasn't right? The same goes for your relationships. If you're honest with yourself, you know in your heart whether a man is right for you or not. Unfortunately it isn't enough to just know. It isn't until you act that change actually takes place. At times people let things cloud their judgment and in turn control their decisions. Some know the reality of their situation but won't act on it because of other factors. Some of those factors many face are their feelings, their emotions, and their desires. To be completely blunt, some of you aren't in love as much as you are in bondage.

You may not be bound physically, but you are bound emotionally and mentally. You see clearly that your attachment to him is hurting you, but you continue to "stick it out" because your emotions are tied to him. You feel that the pain of disconnecting your ties to him is greater than that of putting up with his mistreatment of you. Some of you are in your situation simply because you have allowed yourself to come to the conclusion that even though your relationship isn't where you want it to be, it is the best it can be. Your attachment is more mental than anything else. The minute you believe your situation can't change, it won't. It is important to come to grips with the truth because that's what makes you free. Simply put, freedom is acting on what you believe regardless of outside circumstances, regardless of how you feel, and at times even in spite of what you desire. Don't allow your emotions to keep you tied up in a situation you really don't want to be in. Don't let your feelings cloud your judgment. If you're not careful, in certain instances your feelings can fool you, so it's not good to follow them all the time. A life built on feelings is a life built on sand. It will soon prove to be unstable.

You know what your feelings say, but what does your heart say? There is a difference between the two. Chances are that if you need a million reasons to validate why you are in a particular situation, you probably don't belong there in the first place. It's that simple. We often make things out to be more complicated than they really have to be. In certain instances if we would learn to see things for how they are instead of how we want them to be, life could be a lot easier.

If you're presently in a relationship, I encourage you to examine it. Take it for what it is. Try to block out how you feel and concentrate on what the relationship is rather than what you want it to be. If the situation isn't going how you want it to, ask yourself why. Is this someone with whom you should be involved? If so, why? Regardless of how you feel about him, what does he add to your life? Does he really care for you the way he says he does? Do his actions line up with his words?

I asked some of the women surveyed if they had ever stayed with a man whom they classified as a dog even though they knew he was one. At least half of them answered "yes." When asked why, some said it was because they were trying to look past his shortcomings. Another woman answered, "When you really care for someone, you tend to find all the reasons in the world to stay with them." I have been in relationships where women stuck with me through thick and thin. Sometimes they hung in there even after I violated their trust. In some of those cases I truly cared for those women, and I admire their willingness to stick with me because of the "potential" that they saw in me. However, as a woman it is not your job to see me through to becoming a better man. That process is totally up to me. Perhaps your willingness to let me go will give me a jump start on my own path to change.

Let's take some time to talk about the word *love*. We often use that word so loosely. But let's look at what it really means. This should be a no brainer. Just because a man says that he loves you doesn't mean he really does. He might not be lying to you intentionally. He just may not understand what love really is. He might not know the true attributes of love or how to walk in them to the point where they are actually illustrated in his everyday life. When trying to define love the dictionary will not do. I believe the best place to find the definition of true love is the Bible; "For God so loved the world that he gave his only begotten son" (John 3:16). For Jesus so loved the world that he gave his own life. THAT'S LOVE. Love gives regardless of the cost. To give ourselves on your behalf, that's love. God tells us to love others as we love ourselves. It isn't selfish but rather selfless.

Does your man demonstrate this type of behavior? Do you? If a man says he loves you with his mouth but his actions say he is more interested in pleasing himself, you should know he doesn't love you. Don't allow yourself to become imprisoned while you hope and wait for things to get better. Yes, love is patient. Yes, love is kind. No! Love is not blind. Ignorance is. You don't have to stay in an unfruitful relationship with someone just because you "feel" you love that person. You can leave. It doesn't mean you love him any less. You know the funny misconception about love is that it's a feeling, when in all actuality it isn't. It seems to me that love isn't a feeling but a commitment to a decision. Feelings come and go but love is always steady. It's never wishy-washy. It always remains the same.

When you say you love someone and really mean it, you are committing yourself to treating that person as you would like to be treated on a continual basis. You're committing to treating that person with honor and respect. You are making a decision to be patient with him and to put him before yourself regardless of whether you feel like it or not. That's love.

When you make your man mad and he doesn't put his hands on you, that's love. When you gain a few pounds and he is still faithful to you, that's love. When he cares more about what you want than his own wants, that's love. We must learn to grow in love. So your man may not be exactly there yet. I'm not. If he's trying, that's all that matters. So before the next time you ask, "Are we in love?" think about what we just discussed. Love is a beautiful thing, but don't use it as an excuse to allow yourself to be mistreated. That's not love. Love speaks the truth.

Love yourself enough to tell **you** the truth. It's funny that no matter what topic we review, they all point back to you as an individual. But that's the reality of life. The quality of life you're experiencing right now points back to you. Are you happy with your life right now? If not, you must CHOOSE to act in a manner that will cause change to take place in your life. The first step in the process of change is recognizing the fact that you need to do just that. Sounds simple, but believe me, it's easier said than done.

Most never realize that they need to change because they won't allow themselves to change. They would much rather shove the truth about their situation under the rug and embrace what is essentially a lie. Change can be both uncomfortable and unpleasant but it is absolutely necessary. One will never fix something that one feels has nothing wrong with it. If you are completely satisfied with the quality of your relationships, past or present, great! But if you aren't, you must accept the fact that change has to take place. The pattern of change is this: see it, then embrace it, and lastly do it. Most women want men to change. But it won't happen until they change. Then their life, along with everything involved in it, will follow suit.

"O WHAT A TANGLED WEB WE'VE WOVEN"

What is it that has the power to keep women in unfulfilling relationships? What is it that keeps them connected to someone who is doing nothing whatsoever to help their lives? Why do countless women seem to be trapped, for lack of a better word, in their relationships? Why do so many go back time and time again to a man who is undeserving of their affection? Many women seem to be entangled. It's something that's keeping them connected. It's a connection that is extremely difficult as well as painful to sever. What is it, you ask. What can keep a woman in a place she really doesn't want to be? The answer: SEX. The title of this chapter could have been "The Sex Trap," because in many cases that's exactly what women are engulfed in. In this chapter, we will take a close look at sex. We will talk about its power as well as its purpose. Once we understand its purpose we will likewise understand its power. One thing is for certain, the effects of sexual intercourse last well beyond an orgasm. Later we will look closely at the sexual habits of some but for now let's focus on how sex can ultimately affect you as a woman.

After sex can come emotional attachment and unwanted responsibility. Sex is much more than a three-letter word. Even though many treat it as such, sex is much more than just a physical act. There is a connection that takes place when a man and a woman engage in sexual intercourse. This connection takes place whether the parties involved recognize it or not. Before pornography, before strip clubs, before television and magazines, before the image of what we now perceive to be proper sexual activity was created, there was a man and a woman who never "knew" each other in that way, standing before God, waiting to be pronounced man and wife. At this point they would be known as husband and wife or what we call newlyweds. Even though the two were married, it wasn't considered "official" until the two had sex or consummated the marriage. To consummate means to complete or to finish. To complete what, you may ask. To complete the process and thus to fulfill the purpose of marriage. The purpose of marriage is for two individuals to become one. So in layman's terms, sex is the act in which a man and a woman give themselves one to another and thus become one. When you have sex with a man you're not just giving him your body, but for that period of time you're giving him your mind, your will, your soul and your emotions. In a nutshell you're giving him yourself. When you lie on your back, you are submitting to him. You are vulnerable and defenseless. When you spread your legs you are opening yourself to receive him and all that accompanies him. Who he is, what he has done, and where he's been are becoming a part of you. When you grab him, in essence, you are embracing and accepting the fact that the two of you are becoming one and are being joined. Stop! Think of some of the men with whom you have been in the past. Was it worth it? Were they worthy of you giving yourself to them? The same question applies to your current man if you have one. Is he worth it? What has he done to warrant such a gift from you? What price has he paid? One of the reasons that your man may not value you or your body is because you have given it to him free of charge. The things that we get too easily are the things that we neglect. Ladies, you are no quick thrill or cheap trick. You're priceless. But until you recognize it, no one else will.

When I ask what price a man has paid for you, your affection, your touch, and your intimacy, I'm not speaking in terms of money. We buy things all the time just to throw them away a week later. So money is irrelevant in this equation. What price should a man pay for you, you wonder. He should pay for you with his life.

In the true meaning of marriage when a man says "I do" he is pledging to give you his love, commitment, and attention forever. In essence, he is giving you his life. It is because of this that he now can be trusted with your emotions, your will, your soul, your mind, and your heart. One knows that one can trust a man not based on what he says but based on what he does. No investment, no return. If a man is unwilling to invest himself in you, you should not give yourself to him. **If you don't understand anything else please understand that when you give yourself to a man you give him much more than your body.** I asked several women how they felt after having sex for the first time with a man with whom they were involved. Some said they felt more connected; some said they felt vulnerable. Most of them said they felt closer to him after the fact. The reason they felt closer is because a bond was created.

One must be cautious about to whom one allows oneself to be connected. Many times we don't realize how connected we are to people until we try to pull away from them. A dog doesn't realize that he is bound to a leash until he tries to run away. The same principle applies to your own life. Many women don't realize how much they have invested in a man until they try to pick up and leave.

Be honest. How many times have you said, "I've had it! I'm done with him," only to be back with him a week or two later? If you can relate, raise your hand. Another question I asked the women surveyed was why they stayed in relationships with men who were dogs? Just about all of them said they were comfortable with that particular person in that particular situation. I thought to myself, *How could a situation like that be comfortable?* Then it hit me as I was writing this. In the cases of those women, comfort to them was easy. It was non-confrontational. Comfort spared them from having to deal with reality. If you're not careful, comfort can derail your life. The lives of many suffer because they go after what's comfortable instead of what's best. Trust me. I know it's "uncomfortable" to pull away from someone to whom you have connected yourself. However, if a man is causing the quality of your life to suffer, you will never move forward until you detach yourself from him.

Many are in places that they don't want to be in life because they have allowed their emotions to lead them there. When you become too wrapped up with your emotions, you tend to lose sight of the "big picture." Many are caught up in the "moment," not recognizing that it only takes a "moment" to impact the rest of your life either for good or for bad. This chapter isn't designed to get you to stop having sex with the men you meet; that's ultimately your choice, and you are responsible for everything that follows that choice. This chapter is designed to bring to light the impact sex can have on you as a woman, including the effect it has on your ability to maintain successful relationships.

Some of you may have to learn how to take sex out of the equation. Then maybe, and only maybe, things will begin to add up a little differently. Have you ever wondered why your relationships always seem to hit the same wall? Or why you always seem to enter into relationships with the same type of man? If your relationships aren't turning out as successfully as you like, let me ask, what have you done to change this? The definition of insanity is doing the same thing repeatedly expecting different results. Some of us do this all the time in various areas of our lives. If your relationships haven't been going how you desire, do something different. **I dare you!** What have you got to lose? Maybe some of you should stop having sex so quickly with the men you meet. Others may need to stop having sex altogether. Whatever the case may be, you will never see different results in your life until you begin to do things differently.

Of course it will be uncomfortable at first, but remember the only job of comfort is to keep you where you are. It isn't until you get uncomfortable in your present situation that you will cause your future to change. Nothing in life happens by accident; everything in life is based on cause and effect, which some call sowing and reaping. Your life is the sum total of the seeds that you have sowed so far. Nothing more, nothing less. Every action has a reaction. Countless women continue to put themselves in harmful situations and they continue to bind themselves in relationships that take more from them than add to them. They wonder how and why they have found themselves where they are. They look and blame everybody but themselves. Until they realize the power of their own actions, they will always wind up at the same place no matter how much they try not to. Let me close by saying my goal isn't to convince you to wait until marriage for sex. My goal is to help change the way you look at sex and men, to promote a different thought path concerning the two, and to bring to light the possible effects on you and your relationships.

Chapter 8

GUARD YOUR HEART

In Proverbs 4:23, Solomon wrote, "Keep and guard your heart with all vigilance and above all that you guard, for out of it flow the springs of life." With this statement he was trying to get us to understand how fragile the heart is and what we need to do to protect it. The scripture says *to keep and guard your heart with all vigilance above all that you guard.*

If it wasn't fragile, it wouldn't need to be guarded. If a lot more women would guard their hearts, a lot fewer of them would experience so much heartache and pain.

While I'm not promoting the idea that you be so closed up that it's impossible for a man to connect with you, I am suggesting that you guard your heart by being cautious about whom you let get close to it. Be even more cautious about whom you choose to give it to. Recognize how fragile and important your heart is and act accordingly. The second part of the writing contained in the book of Proverbs states, "for out of it flow the springs of life." The heart isn't just the center of your body; it is the center of your life. Everything in your life revolves around your heart. Everything in your heart will eventually appear in your life. You can give a man your affection and then choose to take it away. You can give him your body, and it leaves when you leave. But once you've given a man your heart you have given him everything. You've just given him your life. Attached to your heart is your life. Once he gets your heart he gets your emotions, your affection, and your body by default. So where is your heart? To how many people have you given a piece of it? Once you give a piece of your heart away, you can never get it back. I don't think a lot of us men or women recognize this. If we did, we would be a lot more careful when dealing with the opposite sex. If your heart were an apple, how much of it would you have left? To whom have you given bits and pieces of it?

We all start with a bright red juicy apple, but over time, relationships, situations, and people chip away at our apple. Some of us have apples that are bruised, some are bitten, and some are barren, stripped to the core. Often when talking to people you can get a sense of the state of their heart. It's funny because those whose apple is at the core guard it for dear life. Women who have reached this point are often suspicious. At times justifiably so. They're angry, but most of all they feel extremely vulnerable. This vulnerability causes them to go to great lengths to "protect" their hearts. As a result, this greatly affects their dealings with men. Getting them to open up can be next to impossible at times. Then there are those women whose apple has not yet been stripped to the core. Instead, their apple has been bitten a little. They are also more cautious when dealing with men, not to the extent of the first set of women, but they are aware of the pain that comes from one's heart getting hurt. They would rather not experience it again. Lastly, there are those who have been blessed to still possess a bright red juicy apple, an apple with little or no spots or blemishes. Some would say that they have the best looking apple of the bunch. This may be true, but ironically they protect theirs the least.

Most people only attempt to preserve what they have when that which they have is almost gone. The key for us as we learn how to guard our heart is to recognize its value. I should apologize. Let us think of the heart not as a red apple but rather as a golden one. It contains the makeup of your life. It's both extremely valuable and fragile at the same time. Guard it and nurture it, but **don't neglect it**. Don't let others abuse it. Some of you do just about everything but make people take a lie detector test before you agree to let them borrow your car. Before handing over the keys, you try to be as confident as possible that the person whom you are about to entrust with your car is responsible enough to treat it the way you would. Many of you only agree to let someone have your car after some careful consideration about their character. How many of you take this same approach when it comes to guarding your heart? Do you observe the actions of men and judge their character before entrusting them with your heart? Or do you just hand over your heart with your fingers crossed, hoping that it doesn't get broken. If the man you have given your heart to does not share in the understanding of how fragile and valuable it is, your heart is in a dangerous place. People often abuse the thing upon which they don't place proper value.

Those things we value the most are those things that we work the hardest to get. So try not to wear your heart on your sleeve so any man with his arms out is able to grab it. I'm not suggesting that you become bottled up and untouchable. I am suggesting that you be cautious and careful to prove that the man in your life is responsible. When going swimming you don't just jump head-first into the water. You test it. You prove it. First you stick your toes in, then your foot, then one leg followed by the other. Only after being assured that the water is suitable to your liking do you submerge yourself into the pool. This method should also somewhat be applied to your relationships. You shouldn't wait until you're in the middle of the swimming pool to discover that the water is too cold. Most of us are too reactive when it comes to relationships. In many cases we don't realize that we are involved with the wrong people until we are attached. By the time we realize that we need to get out of the pool, we're in fifteen feet of water. Once we're attached we rationalize why we should continue to stay attached because at this point it seems to be the easiest thing to do. To avoid these situations you must guard your heart.

The best way to keep your heart from being "broken" is to guard it. A man is only able to break your heart after you've given it to him. I agree there is no way to know the exact outcome of your relationships before they start. However, you can increase your chances of having your relationships be successful by the actions you take. Not only should you be careful about whom you let have your heart, but you must also be careful what you let get in your heart and more importantly what you allow to stay there. Lots of women who have endured heartache at the hands of men have the tendency to allow their hearts to be filled with anger and resentment. When your heart is infected with such things, it poisons your relationships. It continues to do so until it is removed. Resentment about your past will also affect your future. A heart full of resentment is really just a heart full of pain, pain that has since soured.

Resentment doesn't let go. It keeps the pain resident in your heart. Instead of the hurt being removed by your opening up, it closes up the heart. It buries the root of your pain only to allow it to spring up little by little through your actions. Sometimes women push away the "right men" because of how they have been treated by the "wrong men." No matter the past, it is crucial that you keep resentment and bitterness from taking root in your heart. But remember, pain is the precursor to power. It's where you need to be to start over. If you've been hurt before, for your sake you need to forgive, forget, and move on. Why are you still holding on to that situation? Most likely the other person involved isn't. He has gone on with his life. Why haven't you? Life is too short! Live, learn, and grow. If you have experienced some type of heartache, allow it to make you stronger and wiser. Don't allow it to cripple you by holding on. Don't allow it to hinder your future relationships. Some of you are mad at the entire male gender because of your experience with a few men. I don't discount your past, or your future for that matter, but life happens. Don't let a few dark spots in your past rob you of a bright future.

Some of you may have good men in your lives. You just haven't recognized it. Some of you may have good men pursuing you, but you're pushing them away because of a past experience. Some of you are using the excuse, "I just need my space." If that's true, that's great. In many cases that's just a cover-up to the fact that you have allowed yourself to get to the point in which it's hard for you to trust a man. It's impossible for you to go back and rearrange your past. Even if you could, you would be a totally different person today. My advice to you is to move on. If you aren't used to guarding your heart, now is the time to begin. It's never too late. I guarantee that if you begin to be more careful with your heart, your relationships with men will improve as a result. You also will be less likely to get hurt. Prove those men who are in pursuit of you. Not just once but on a continual basis.

If you ever want to truly find out the type of man you are involved with, pay attention to his habits. His habits serve as a self-portrait of his character. Keep in mind that none of us are perfect. However, the habits of a man will show you the direction in which his life is heading. If you're attached to him, your life will sooner or later go in the same direction his is heading, whether it is up or down. Show me where your heart is, and I'll show you where your life is. If you don't like the quality of your life, including those who surround it, examine the quality of your heart. There is a huge difference between a heart that's guarded and one that's closed. Those who guard their hearts are careful, while those who close theirs do so out of fear. Fear keeps you in bondage. If you're so afraid of getting hurt again that you keep your heart closed up, that's a sign that you have yet to get over your past. Until you deal with them, the effects from your previous relationships will hinder your present ones. Decide, from this moment forward, to guard your heart. Commit to nurturing it. If you do you won't regret it. Take care of your heart, and your heart will take care of you.

WHAT DO YOU WANT
FROM ME?

I mean that literally. Though I'm not referring to me specifically, I am referring to men in general. Once you establish what it is you are looking for in a man, it makes your dealings with him *cut and dried*. By expecting a man with whom you are to be involved to possess certain qualities, you will easily be able to recognize if what you are looking for is absent. If you refuse to expect anything you will accept anything. A lot of you wouldn't be in relationships that you're presently in if you really established what you wanted in a man. I asked several women to describe a "good man." I asked them to tell me about some of the characteristics that they thought a good man should have. Some of those mentioned were loyalty, honesty, and dependability. I'm pretty sure that most of you would name some similar qualities when describing what you feel to be qualities of a "good man." How many of you can honestly say that those qualities are present in your man? If he doesn't possess such characteristics, why is that? If you want such qualities in a man, why doesn't your man have them? The reason: There is a huge difference between wanting something and looking for something. Example, I may want a new job, but until I start looking for one, I will never find it.

Do you understand the difference? In this case to look for something also means to expect or require it. You will never get what you want until you look for it. Let's make a list of the qualities that were most commonly mentioned when I talked to women much like you.

The top five qualities were:

- Honesty: upright; just; free from fraud
- Responsibility: of good credit or position
- Dependability: reliable
- Trustworthiness: able to be believed in
- Motivation: passionate about something greater than oneself

Based on this short list, are any of these qualities present in your man? If not, you may want to re-evaluate your situation. Can you imagine if companies just hired people at random, without first requiring that applicants possess specific qualifications? Many companies would fold, not because those hired were "bad" people, but rather because they were a bad fit for the position in which they were placed. The lives of many women are folding because of the men they have allowed to gain positions in their lives. Granted, it takes time to learn a person's true character. However, there ought to be certain traits you look for from the beginning when first meeting a man.

Once you establish what you're looking for, in many situations you will be able to tell if a man fits that description after having just a few conversations. It only takes a few conversations to discover a person's faith and some of his goals and aspirations. You can even get a small view of his outlook on life if you pay attention. You must learn to listen to a man's heart instead of his mouth. His mouth is capable of telling you what you want to hear, but his heart will always reveal what's in it. Once you realize what you want in a man, his words become irrelevant to a certain extent. Of course you want to pay attention to his conversation, but even more you want to make sure his actions are in line with his words. If not, then you may have a fraud on your hands.

I recommend that you write down a small list of some qualities you would like your man to possess. This list should contain immediate qualities, surface qualities that are recognizable immediately. These include qualities that will either support or hinder the quality of your relationships. One such quality could be a person's faith, which may govern his actions. It also could be whether he is a heavy drinker or if he likes to party a lot. You aren't trying to determine whether he is a good or bad person. Your goal is to determine whether he is a good or bad fit for you compared to your lifestyle and your personality. If you don't settle these issues before you enter into a relationship, it will hinder the relationship's full potential. What you learn about a man on the first date can often determine if there ought to be a second one. Some may find that to be mean, but I find it to be a reality. There's no need to keep moving forward with someone who isn't right for you. Just because a man isn't good for you doesn't mean he isn't a good man. It just means he isn't a good man for you.

With that said, you shouldn't start pushing people away if they aren't what you're looking for. There are different types of relationships. All male/female relationships don't have to have a romantic link. You first must know what you want. If you're just looking for friends and desire to meet new people, then it is absolutely essential that you be open-minded. But if you are looking for a man with whom you wish to become romantically involved, you need to be specific.

Let's talk about balance regarding this subject. Most of us take things to either one extreme or the other. The key to a prosperous life is balance. This is also the key to a successful relationship. Earlier we talked about making a list, whether written or mental, of the qualities you want in a man. I bet some of your lists are like a book, while others' lists are a few words. You see, some women expect too much from men while others expect too little. Even though their levels of expectance are different, their expectations continue to yield the same results. They both have the same dilemma. They are not receiving what they expect and are unfulfilled and unsatisfied as a result of it.

The one who expects too much is doing one of two things. One, she is either looking for something she will never find, or two, she is expecting immediate progress in an area that needs time to grow. Let's concentrate on the first point. We covered this somewhat in an earlier chapter. First, you must remember people will let you down. We are all human and prone to making mistakes. Second, men are not your source of fulfillment. If you believe so, there will always be a void in your life. Now that we've covered that, let's look at some of the more surface things.

We always say things like "nobody's perfect," but we don't always act that way. I mean that in terms of the expectations we place on others. I can be the first to admit that there are times when I place very high expectations on those with whom I am in relationship. When they don't perform to the level I think they should, I become frustrated at times and consequently dissatisfied with the relationship. The funny thing is, it's never the actions of the other person that cause my frustration and lack of fulfillment but rather my own expectations. In the world in which we live today, people are looking for instant gratification. We want things to just appear and disappear as we please. Sadly, many take the same approach when it comes to their relationships. Many want a return without first investing. But like anything else, relationships take time to grow. Character develops over time. Some women sometimes miss out on golden opportunities because they are looking for "Prince Charming." There is nothing wrong with that, but some of you searching for "Prince Charming" may already have a prince in your presence. He just might not be as charming as you would like: YET.

Flowers don't bloom overnight. It takes time for a caterpillar to transform into a butterfly. If you have a man who has the ESSENTIAL qualities that you are looking for and you keep sowing proper seeds in your relationship, you will ensure that you receive a harvest. That doesn't mean that you should continue to invest your life in a "dud." That's the reason you should establish what it is you're looking for. Once you realize that, you can easily identify a "dud" from a "stud." Many times we expect so much of others and so little of ourselves. This shouldn't be. This is where a proper balance comes into play. For many women, their situation is the complete opposite. The bar of expectation for many is set too low. They don't expect anything, and as a result they will accept anything. Many often settle in life only to later complain about the very thing that they've settled for. **You will never receive life's best if you don't go after it.** Don't just settle for any man. *Wait for life's best.* I don't mean wait as in sitting on the couch expecting "Mr. Right" to drop out of the sky. Expect it! Prepare for it! If you want "Mr. Right," become "Ms. Right" first. Also get a mental picture of life's best so that you may recognize it when it shows up.

MAN PLEASER

The *Merriam-Webster* definition of the word *please* is "to make happy or satisfied." In terms of your relationship, there's absolutely nothing wrong with you making a man happy and/or satisfied. In fact you should do just that. But in fact he should also do that for you. When I mention the words "man pleaser," I am referring to motive more than anything else. Often the reason we do something is just as important as the action itself. As a man I think there are too many women who are "man pleasers." This type of characteristic is displayed in several ways. Some women do things specifically to catch the attention of men; some do things to get a particular guy to "like" them or to commit to them, and others do things to keep a guy from leaving them. In these particular situations, motives have gone astray, causing some women to do things that are out of their character to get attention and in some cases affection from men. Unfortunately, the type of attention and affection they are looking for they never receive. Are you a man pleaser? Do you do things solely to gain the attention and affection of men? If so, why? What good is attention and so-called affection if you have to strip yourself of your dignity to receive it? That doesn't seem like a fair trade to me. A lot of women engage in sexual activity not because they want to, but because they think that if they give their bodies they will receive the affection they desire in return. Most of them never do.

Men often pick up on this tendency some women have, and many exploit it. I can personally testify to this because I've done it. I have run into women who for whatever reason deemed my attention and affection to be valuable. Why? I don't know. But once I realized what they were doing, I took advantage of it. I was able to get them to do things that they normally wouldn't go along with, but because they were trying to "win" my affection, they agreed. I would show them just enough attention and display just enough affection for me to get what I wanted when I wanted it, whether it be sex, money, or something else. Men are sometimes smarter than women think. I would strategically call and text the women in my life saying things like "I miss you" or " I was thinking about you" so that I could be certain that I could get what I wanted out of them. In most cases it worked. I'm sure most of you would say that you would never act in such a manner. The interesting thing is, so would the women of whom I took advantage if you were to ask them. Most aren't able to see their shortcomings until someone points them out to them.

This is the purpose of this chapter. My motivation for writing this book was the hope that women would be inspired as well as empowered to change their lives. I was specifically prompted to write this chapter because of a particular situation that took place in my own life.

I met a female who happened to be a very nice person. She had a good head on her shoulders and was a very sweet girl. I would even venture to say that she was a rare breed, so to speak. She was a homebody. She was the type to cook and clean. She had the desire to really take care of her man. We went out a few times, talked on the phone, and got to know each other. After a while it became apparent that she had become fond of me. However, at this point in my life I was focused on other things. And, for whatever reason, I was not looking at her in that way. She let me know that she was interested in me. Not only did she let me know but she'd do things to try to make me interested in her on the level she was into me. She would say things like, "What don't you like about me?" or "Why don't you want me?" She wanted attention and affection from me that I was unwilling to give her. She did things for me that she didn't have to do and should not have done. She gave me things I didn't deserve. In doing so she put herself in an extremely vulnerable position. I will be the first to admit that I could have acted more responsibly but I didn't. That's proof that you shouldn't count on someone else to do for you what you ought to do for yourself. At this point however I did have enough integrity to not take total advantage of the young lady. It wouldn't have been hard to do. She basically gift wrapped her body for me.

The dangerous part wasn't that she was vulnerable; it was that she was oblivious to the fact. That made her situation a dangerous one. Many of you reading this book may have a few of these tendencies and could be in a similar situation. Some of you are doing things to try and get a man. You are cooking for him, buying him things, giving him your body, all to convince him that you are deserving of his affection. If you have to convince him to care about you, then you need to leave him alone. On the other side of the spectrum, there are also those who do things to try and keep a man. Not only do they do things to ensure that he stays around; they also put up with things to be sure that they don't lose the attention and affection they have gained. If you are involved in such a dilemma begin to question the motives behind why you really do what you do. If more of us would just ask ourselves why we are doing what we're doing before acting and answer HONESTLY, many of our outcomes would be significantly different.

The key is to be honest with yourself. If you can't do this, you will never uncover the truth about your life. As a matter of fact, let's begin right now. The last time you had sex, why did you do it? Why did you do it with that particular person? Did you find what you were looking for (beyond physical pleasure)? Why are you in the relationship that you are in? Why are you still with a man whom you don't trust? Stop.... I hope you take your time and really answer those questions honestly for your sake. As you answer, begin to think about how your situation might have been different had you posed those questions before you engaged in the activities I previously mentioned. If you began to realize your situation would be different, don't feel badly. You haven't done anything that anybody else can't relate to. This chapter isn't to condemn you but rather to inform you. Your life will change as soon as you begin to do things differently.

"Groupie Luv"

Let's now dive into another subject that lies under the central thought of this chapter. Let's talk about "groupie luv." This really could've been a chapter in its own right, but I thought it to be a by-product of the overall theme, "man pleaser." Essentially groupies are nothing more than "man pleasers." What is a groupie? *Webster's* defines groupies as young women who follow rock groups around on the road. However, that isn't all there is to the word. In fact, the word actually means and symbolizes much more.

My definition of a groupie is a woman who values a man's attention more than her own self-respect. We men view these types of women in a certain way. When most of us think of a groupie we think of someone who is easy, a woman who will allow a man of certain "status" to basically do anything he wants to them. Groupies are at the bottom of the totem pole. They are women who get no respect from men whatsoever. Quite frankly, they are only as good as what it is they're willing to give up. Let me pose this question to you. Are you a groupie? I'm positive 99.9 percent of you will answer "no" to that question. However, I would like to challenge that "statistic."

How many of you have ever said, "Girl, if I ever met Trey Songz I would give him some" or "If I see Brad Pitt I'm going do this to him" or "just let me meet Denzel... I'm going to make him forget all about his wife"? If this is you, don't raise your hand. Someone may find out. Well, I'm sorry to inform you, but if you answered "yes" to any of those questions, you are not as far from "groupie" status as you may think. I admit I find women to be extremely complicated. There are many things that I have yet to comprehend concerning the female persuasion. Even with all that, this subject is the kicker for me. I cannot understand how so many women can throw themselves at men solely because of their "status" in life. I will never understand how a woman can allow a man (no matter what status he holds) to cause her to look like (I'm trying to be nice) a flat-out whore. Since when does a hefty bank account give a man the right to treat you as if you're nothing? Is your favorite rapper, actor, or whatever that much more special than the guy making fifty grand a year? Does fame and fortune entice you that much? It's ironic that the fame and fortune that allows him to do what he pleases with you is the same fame and fortune that you will never see a piece of.

After he's done he moves on to the next city as you go home a "better" woman because you were "pimped" by a celebrity. You're thinking, *Wow, I just slept with a superstar,* while he's telling his friends, "I can't believe she let me do that to her," as someone asks, "Who was she?" and he answers, "I don't know, some groupie."

Let me encourage you that if you're going to live to please anyone, let it be God. Men come and go. The next time you do something for a man, whatever it may be let it be because you care for him and you genuinely want him to be happy. Don't do things for him because you want him to give you his attention and affection. Make it a habit to monitor your motives. Let me say it again YOU DO NOT NEED A MAN. Once you settle that within yourself you will no longer do things to get one.

From Me To You: A Side Note

I know there are a lot of bold statements and even declarations in this book. I'm sure that there have been one or more instances while reading that you have said, "That's easy for you to say." I'm almost certain that many of you have said, "How can you truly understand my situation? You're a man!" That I am, and I cannot deny that fact. The truth is, however, I see daily where we men come up short in being there for you the way we should. I have witnessed the tears of heartache from countless women after learning that their man has cheated on them. I have even been at fault on numerous occasions. With all this said I am now convinced that it doesn't have to be this way. It shouldn't be for that matter. I know I say things like "If he isn't treating you right, leave him alone." I make bold statements such as, "Make men respect you." I encourage you not to tolerate being lied to and cheated on anymore. I can see where some may think I am implying that the task at hand is an easy one. I am not! I know it's hard. It's challenging, it's new, and it's different from how you may have operated in the past. Think about this however. Life itself is challenging. Nothing in life worth having comes easily. So in order to move beyond what we are currently experiencing into a better way of living, we must overcome resistance. I hope and I pray that you are up for the challenge. Your quality of life depends on it.

Chapter 11

NEVER SETTLE!

This is one of the most important chapters in this book, if not the most important one. What makes this subject so vital is the potential it has to impact your entire life. Some things once implemented into your life will affect every area of it. Some understand this and some do not. There are two types of people in life. Some say that there are the rich and the poor. Others say the fortunate and the less fortunate. But I submit to you that even with all of that, there are those who settle and those who don't. It's that simple. There are those who simply take life as it comes and then there are those who participate in the direction their life goes. Most never get what they want out of life because they settle for what they have. They only go after what seems to be available. Success in life shouldn't be measured by money and material possessions. The truly successful are those who live life to its fullest potential, those who make the most of every day that they have. They focus on progress and are able to minimize distractions. These are the truly successful.

Most who settle don't realize that they are doing so. They have come to the point at which they believe that where they are and what they see is all that's available. Let's relate this topic to you specifically as a woman. A lot of you reading this book have settled in many areas of your life. You've settled for what you thought were the only options available to you. Everything that you've gained so far from this book will amount to nothing if you continue to settle. You would solve a lot of your relationship woes if you just stopped settling. Yes, you should know what you're looking for. It doesn't stop there. The majority of people know what it is they want, but only a minority actually possess it. There have been countless times while knowing full well the type of woman I was looking for, I settled simply for what was available at the moment. The need for instant gratification feeds our desire to settle. Instead of waiting for the best, most simply settle for the next best thing. Some may not agree, but I believe that there is a good man for every woman who desires one. Even if you haven't met one yet, it doesn't mean that there are none at all. I'll bet a few over time have crept in and out of your life without notice. Sometimes when you put so much focus on the glitter you miss the gold.

Just because he looks good and smells good it doesn't mean he is good. It's funny that most of the people after they have settled tend to complain about the very thing that they have settled for. There are different reasons why we settle in different areas of our lives. Impatience is one of the biggest reasons. Some of you are planning to get married solely because you're tired of not being married. You may feel like the odd ball out of the bunch because all of your friends are married. So instead of waiting for the ideal mate, you hook up with the one who is ideal at the moment. You rationalize it to yourself. You think because you're getting "older" your time is running short. I beg to differ. There is never an excuse to justify settling. Others settle not because of a lack of patience but a lack of vision: "Where there is no vision the people perish" (Proverbs 29:18). Simply put, a vision is a clear picture of exactly where you want to be in the future. The future can be tomorrow, next month, a year from now, or even five years down the road. Some see further ahead than others; this is why some end up further ahead in life. A vision concentrates not on what you have but rather on what you want to have. Get a mental picture of where you want your life to be. Once you have it, pursue it passionately and don't stop until it becomes a reality for you. Without a clear picture of the direction we want our lives to go in, it is hard to focus on the future. For this reason, many of us tend to live as if today is all that matters. Then we live by impulse instead of weighing our decisions against our desired future. Create a vision, embrace it, and never settle. This applies to your life in general, not just regarding men. Some of you have settled for men who you know aren't right for you, men who have hurt you more than they will ever help you. When you allow things to take place in your life that shouldn't be, you have settled. When you put up with cheating and physical abuse, among other things, you have settled.

When you entertain men with no ambition at all, you possibly lose your own. You have settled. When you have become content with being his "baby mamma" and not his wife, you have settled. It's not just the way things are, it's the way you've allowed them to be. I've heard women say things like "men will be men" to excuse the behavior of their significant other. That's bull! It's an excuse that will keep you where you are as long as you continue to make it. He is who you allow him to be. Your life is where you have allowed it to go. Don't settle anymore. Get the best out of life. Go after God's best in every area of your life. You were not born just to have babies and cook, even though some of you may behave like it. Your life has so much more value and potential. Don't allow your past to rob you of your future. If you are a single young mother who was forced to leave school to take care of your child, stay encouraged. Life is full of detours. The key is learning how to stay on the path. If you keep running the race, you will eventually make it to your finish line. You can go back to school if you desire. Learn how to overcome your circumstances. Some of us have an easier journey but we all have the ability to be successful. Make your life a success, according to your definition of it. Remind yourself daily that "all things are possible to him [or her] who believes" (Mark 9:23). If you want to be rich, then do so. If you want to be famous, then do so. If you want a good job, a nice car, and a house independent of any man's involvement, go after it. **Don't stop until your dreams become real.**

Once you make it a habit not to settle, it will spread to other areas of your life and increase the quality of it by default. Take a look at your life. Evaluate it. Examine it in detail. Include your house, your car, your bank account, and your man. Are you content with where you are and with the direction you're heading? Do you have the desires of your heart? Can you do better? If the answer is *yes*, then do better. Don't settle for an unfaithful man when you can have a committed one. Don't settle for an apartment when you can have a house. It's good to be grateful and you should be. But never allow yourself to become complacent. The moment you do your life stops moving forward and begins to head in reverse. Things either get better or get worse: *there is no in-between.* If your man isn't faithful now, he won't be six months from now. Don't fool yourself. Time doesn't make men become better men. Our actions do. It is time to change. If you lack financially you will continue to do so until you learn the habits of those who are financially prosperous.

In short, your life won't change until you do. Nothing happens by osmosis. He may have said that he wouldn't cheat anymore or that he would never hit you again; this may prove to be true for a week or so. But if his habits haven't changed, believe things will ultimately return to how they were previously. The question is, *Will you still settle for that?*

Remember, there are those who settle and those who don't. Which one of the two are you? Why live life if you can't get the most out of it? You don't have to continue to engage in an unfruitful relationship. Stop sitting on life's sidelines and get into the game. Just because you're a lady doesn't mean that you have to be a cheerleader. Realize your value in life and fulfill your full potential. Get what you want out of life without having to compromise. Remember, there is more to life than what you see. Go after the desires of your heart. Get the man you want. Drive the car you want. Live in the house you want. Live the life you want. As singles we should be successful in our own right. We ought not to be depending on our connection to another to determine our success in life. Life is what we make it. <u>Make yours the best</u>!

Chapter 12

NO STRINGS ATTACHED:
THE NEW PHENOMENON

For as long as I can remember, I have been fascinated by the inter-action between men and women. I can remember wondering as a teenager if the way that I interacted with females would be different when I moved into adulthood. Surprisingly I found out that things were relatively the same. Instead of talking about school, we talked about jobs and careers. Instead of inquiring about the number of siblings, I now inquire about the number of children. The format is pretty much unchanged. One thing has changed, however, and that is the level of our interaction regarding the physicality of our relationships.

I can remember meeting girls as a teenager, and as most young boys do when they are dealing with raging hormones, I would try to calcu-late how long it would take for us to have sex. It used to be that sex was seen as okay if it was within a committed relationship. So in high school most girls made you wait a few months before agreeing to allow sexual intercourse. That was if you were lucky. Sex was always a topic among my conversations as a teen. For my friends and me growing up, it seemed elusive and was a big deal if you were actually doing "It." As I got older I noticed that sex became easier to come by. It went from being okay to have sex within a committed relationship to being okay just to have sex.

I mention all of this because in today's world, for many, sex is not what it used to be. It is not as exclusive as it once was. We now live in a free society that employs the motto "If it feels good, do it." I'm not preaching but just wondering if this is how we really ought to live. While relationships seem to be at an all-time low, sexual activity seems to be at an all-time high, especially among non-committed singles. Going back to my beginning illustration, I can remember there was a time when a girl wouldn't dare think of becoming intimate with me before she had some type of commitment from me. Those days seem to be gone. Now as a single, a good majority of the women whom I meet are willing to engage in sexual intercourse with me long before a relationship is even brought up. Is this wrong? Is it immoral? What about this idea of having sex outside of a committed relationship? Is sex with no strings attached harmful? Is it even possible? I asked several women what they thought about these ideas and here is what they had to say.

Woman #1:

Having sex outside of a committed relationship is not for everyone. It can cause problems, and often people get hurt if the lines of communication are not open. I think that it's okay sometimes as long as both people know and understand the situation. Through personal experiences, I know first-hand that things can become complicated because sooner or later feelings seem to get involved. As women we give part of ourselves away when we have sex. So I do think we should be skeptical about with whom we lie down.

Woman #2:

I think sex outside of a relationship unfortunately is normal. Relationships are not what they used to be, and people still have the urge to have sex, so why not have casual sex? However, sex with no strings attached does not work. As long as two people are having sex on a continual basis there are going to be some feelings involved.

Woman #3

I don't see anything wrong with having sex with no strings attached, and I do believe that there can be such a thing. If you are not looking for a committed relationship, then more or less you are looking for something more physical and less emotional. If you know yourself, you know whether or not you can detach yourself emotionally from a physical situation. If you're able to handle your emotions, then more than likely you will be okay with just a physical relationship.

Woman #4

No sex outside of a committed relationship! Women should be more honest with themselves; there are always strings attached when two people escalate their relationship. My only suggestion to women is that they HOLD OUT, not as a punishment to men, but as a reward for themselves.

Those were not my words, but rather those were the words of your peers. They came from the hearts of women who have similar thoughts, familiar emotions, and many of the same desires that you have. Many of you can relate to one or more of those thoughts. Some share in the belief that sex outside of a committed relationship is fine. Some believe that it is normal for consenting adults to engage in such activities and in essence believe that it is merely a sign of the world we live in. Still others of you may agree more with Woman #4, who sternly stated that there should be no sex outside of a committed relationship. Whatever your point of view, the goal is to find out the truth behind why we do what we do. We do so to discover if there is a better way to go about leading our lives. Once this is done, it is up to each of us individually to decide the path down which we will take our lives.

This chapter is different in that we are not simply looking for a solution; we are intensely in search of the truth. It is the truth that we know has the ability, power, and potential to make us free. It is indeed up to each of us if we choose to accept such freedom and walk in the power that liberty brings about. With that said, what then shall we do? If we continue on the same path we are currently on, it may lead us to a place that we do not want to be. As stated before we must FIRST decide where we want to be. Once we do this, we can move our lives forward effectively and efficiently. The things that we do in the present will ultimately affect our future in some way. Because of this we must value every opportunity we have to choose. Everything that we have and ever will have is a gift from God. It is what we do with each gift given to us that matters. Our bodies, our minds, and our time are all gifts from our creator. We ought to be good stewards of all that which has been placed in our hands.

If you and I would begin to see our bodies as gifts, we might not give them away so easily. You see, with each gift that we receive comes the ability to give that gift to another. We have been given time, and we in turn have the ability to choose to whom we would like to give our time or with whom we would like to spend our time. The same goes for our bodies. We can freely give them away to whom we choose. However, just because we have this ability does not mean that we should always exercise it. Or does it?

Let's speak candidly about uncommitted sexual relations and how men look at them. Sex outside of a committed relationship is a man's dream come true! Sounds funny, but it is the truth. We can get what we are ultimately looking for without having to put in the usual effort required. That effort may consist of getting our feelings involved, taking you out on dates, and being monogamous or at least appearing to be. A committed relationship usually consists of us spending our money, and giving up a lot of our time, and it requires us to be attentive to you as a woman. So when you tell us as men that we can get the reward without having to fight the battle, in most cases, we jump at the opportunity. An acquaintance of mine recently remarked, "Sex has become one of the easiest things in the world to get: what the hell happened to the chase? I thought women knew we liked that".

For the majority of men, sex plays a part in how we interact with women. Would you like to test that statement? If you are in a relationship and are having sex on a somewhat regular basis with your partner, inform him that you guys will not be having sex for an extended period of time, and I guarantee that you will see a difference in your relationship immediately. This is even true for those men who are celibate. Do you think that they would be getting married if there was no sex involved? This isn't to suggest that sex is all we think or care about as men, even though I can admit that it often seems that way. The truth, however, is that it does play a factor in how we interact with you as a woman. As men, for the most part, we are used to sex meaning more to you than it does to us. For many men sex is a mere physical act. Evidence of sex meaning more to you as a woman than it does to me as a man is the fact that we men are generally more free in our sexual nature in that we tend to give our bodies away with little regard at times. This is true especially compared to the traditional sexual behavior of women.

So when you illustrate to me that I can have your body without first committing to you what you are essentially communicating to me is that you do not think of sex as being important enough that a commitment needs to be established first before we engage in it. Commitment is more than just a few words. Commitment can be seen through actions often forged by emotions. It's an attachment that is beyond the superficial. There are married men who are still uncommitted. It is more than saying "I do." More than anything else, commitment is a continuous investment. Once a man receives the signal from you that such an investment is not required, it may be harder to get him to commit to you after sex takes place. If by chance he does, it could be even more difficult to get him to be monogamous on a consistent basis. It's like giving a kid dessert before dinner. For some of us when we were younger, the only way our mothers could convince us to eat all of our dinner, which normally included some type of vegetable, was to include the promise that if we would do so, we would be rewarded at the end with desert. We had to put up with the sour so that we could enjoy the sweet.

So when you tell us that you are fine with casual sex by agreeing to sexual intercourse before any kind of commitment or emotional attachment/investment takes place on our part please do not be upset if the effort we put into the relationship is casual. What you put in is what you get out, and what you allow you will most definitely receive. A man will only treat with value what he sees as being valuable to him. This goes back to you as a woman having the power in your possession. We don't make you valuable. Therefore it isn't in our ability to increase or diminish your value. You are as valuable as you see yourself being. As men we simply treat your body how you allow us to treat it. If you're going to be in the driver's seat, you might as well steer the car where you want to go. Once again, I encourage you that you are in control. Is your body worth a commitment? Could it be worth even more than a temporary commitment but a lifelong one sealed by a wedding ring? Those are questions that only you can answer. Those answers, however, will affect your dealings with every man you meet.

No Strings Attached

I separated these two sections because I feel that even though they can be interconnected they are still separate in many ways. To me, sex outside of a committed relationship isn't necessarily sex with no strings attached. There are different types of instances in which individuals engage in sexual activity. Some do so with people they may be dating and others have random partners at times. So what does *sex with no strings attached* mean? Does it work? Of course I asked around. The first woman I asked answered as follows:

Sex with no strings attached is you getting it on with someone but once you leave that bedroom you are not obligated to him nor is he obligated to you. Both parties have a clear understanding that we are not together. I currently cannot invest the time it takes to make a relationship work, but I still have needs! I long for that affection that comes with having that special someone.

I wonder if any of her thoughts were comparable to that of your own. Before we decide that, let's look at how another woman answered the same question. Here are her thoughts that she was gracious enough to share with us:

NO! Sex with no strings attached never works. One always becomes emotionally involved. I feel like there will always be complications. You can lay out the rules: no sleeping over, no dining out, blah, blah, blah. Let's face it, if you are having good sex with someone you are going to get a little caught up. Jealousy starts to creep in. One person now wants to know the other's whereabouts and if they are sexually involved with other people, which in most cases they are because no relationship has been established.

As we can see when it comes to these particular subjects, everyone seems to have her own opinion. Some are similar and some differ. Some seem to be more traditional, while others in their opinions seem to be more new age. While writing this chapter I thought it would be productive to switch it up a little. This whole book thus far has essentially been about you. In fact the majority of this chapter specifically focuses on your thoughts and opinions as women. However, it may be even more effective if you could read some thoughts straight from the minds of men. So I posed the same questions we went over earlier to several men --- men of various ages and races, some single and some currently in committed relationships. I asked one man what he thought about sex with no strings attached, and here is his response:

I think it's cool. But neither party involved should expect respect now or later. Even with that, it's rarely no strings attached anyway. There is always that awkward feeling of Should I call her the next day? *I could never be in a committed relationship with someone I'm having this type of involvement with. I wouldn't be able to give of myself fully.*

That's not all. Here is what another man said when I asked him for his thoughts on sex outside of a committed relationship:

I find it to be absolutely normal. We are adults; it is what we do.

I asked this same man if he ever had been or thought he could be in a committed relationship with a woman who permits this type of interaction. Here is what he had to say:

Well, I'm not sure; it may be kind of hard. If I'm getting sex from a woman without having to commit, I think it would take me longer to agree to be in a monogamous relationship with her. We don't necessarily need to be a couple, but I think she should at least make me wait a month or two.

I can hear you screaming, "Double standard!!!" Yes, it is. However, with that said, the sole purpose of this section is to shed some light on how men think regarding this subject. Before concluding things, let's hear what a few more men had to say on the topic.

I asked another man what he thought about sex with no strings attached; his reasoning was this:

If both parties are okay with it, I think that it is fine. If the girl wants to have sex with no strings attached, that's fine, and it doesn't make her easy in my eyes. But that's on a case-by-case basis. If she were to be having sex with me and other men simultaneously, then she would be a slut in my eyes.

This is what one final man had to say when I posed similar questions to him:

Well, morally I definitely think that it is wrong. Outside of that, I think you really have to be careful about who you sleep with, because there is so much out there these days. For me, it's sex minus a genuine emotional attachment that would cause my perception of a female to be altered. I think a woman's body is one of the most precious gifts that a man could receive, and if she were to give it to me too easily, say just after one night, I would find it hard to respect her. Women essentially deal the cards; we just play the hand. We can only do to them what they let us.

Did you read that, ladies? Several of these men have echoed a point I have been determined to drive home throughout this book. It is this: We men can only do to women what **they** let us do.

In my personal experience there has always been an empty/shallow feeling left behind after engaging in sexual intercourse with someone with whom I shared no emotional attachment. When it is meaningless, it definitely feels that way. That feeling afterwards may not affect your body, but it definitely impacts your soul. A commitment signals an investment, and the greater the commitment, the greater the investment. The greater the investment, the more you are liable to reap from it. Casual sex, though often pleasurable in the moment, is fleeting in the long term. Many times the empty feeling that I was left with after the act was committed lasted longer than the pleasure I experienced from the act itself.

Whether you think casual sex is right or wrong, there is no disputing the fact that it is very dangerous in today's society. Sexually transmitted diseases are running rampant within our communities, and women are being infected at an alarming rate with diseases such as herpes, gonorrhea, and AIDS just to name a few. We only get one body, so it is to our best advantage that we treasure it the best we can. If you lie down with just anybody, you are liable to get up with anything. That goes for all of us---men and women, which includes you and me. As a woman you control whom you allow to enter your body. If you are going to be having sex, especially if it's casually, you need to be using protection, i.e., a CONDOM. However, remember even they aren't 100 percent safe. They do break.

In my adult life I can say that as high as 90 percent of the women with whom I've had sexual relations never asked if I had a condom, let alone required it before-hand. Most just took their clothes off and lay in the bed with the lights off, vulnerable and open. It seemed as if they were leaving the condom part up to me. In fact on a few occasions I was asked by women to take the condom off during sex. Some of these women barely knew me, and even the ones who did never actually saw my test results. Let's not allow our desire for pleasure to derail our present and shipwreck our future. Be smart and be safe.

I know there was a lot mentioned in this chapter, so let's attempt to tie it all together and see if we can end with a new thought path. To some, sex outside of marriage is wrong. Others may believe that sex outside of a committed relationship is wrong. Still others believe that sex is just part of who we are and we should enjoy it as we please. Whatever your beliefs, thoughts, and opinions on the subject, they are important in that they help to determine your ideal. By ideal I mean how you truly desire things to be. That is what most of us are after. We are after our ideal mate, ideal career, and ideal home amongst other things. The choice is now yours regarding the path you take in your life. Each of us must decide if we will start on a new journey or continue down the same path as before. Whatever direction we decide to go, we must do so with knowledge and understanding. We must be honest with ourselves to determine whether or not we are up for the challenge of obtaining the true desires of our hearts. Some want a happy marriage. Some simply want a healthy monogamous relationship. Whatever it is that your heart truly yearns for, I encourage you to pursue, expect, and even wait for it. Even more, I pray that you will not settle for anything **LESS** than your ideal.

IT'S ALL ABOUT YOU

Yes, ladies, it's true! You are finally the center of attention. It's all about you! In case you didn't know this, it's always been all about you. Your life, your relationships, etc., are all about you. You deserve to be exactly where you are in life. You deserve everything you've gotten so far. Again your life is your responsibility. Whether you choose to accept that responsibility or not is up to you. So in that case I admonish you to live life on your terms. However you want your life to be lived, LIVE IT. Sometimes we make our lives too complex. We allow too many "outside" circumstances to affect the quality of our lives. As a result, most of us focus the majority of our attention and efforts on the outside. When we fail to see significant change, we become frustrated. Our lack of success at changing our outside circumstances has led many of us to believe that things are how they are and can't be any other way. Many may believe this, but that still doesn't make it true. If you want what's going on outside you to change, you must first address what's going on inside you. It is the only way.

Once you begin to address your inside situation, your outside one will begin to look different. For example, you can't stop it from raining, but you can surely keep from having the rain come into your living room. Imagine someone becoming so frustrated at their couch getting wet that they go outside with a bucket trying to catch the raindrops attempting to keep their furniture from being ruined. In this case they are focused on the outside problem and oblivious to the inside solution. The simple thing would be for them to just patch the roof. I have already said it, but let me reiterate it. Most of you have yet to realize the power that you have. I've met very few women who actually exercise such power. When it comes to relationships, many women just allow things to happen and then react based on how those things have affected them. Living this way is like a non-stop roller coaster ride. One day you're up, the next day you're down. Seems like a lousy way to live, but that's the story of some people's lives. Instead of getting life's best, you continuously receive its leftovers. If you are tired of scraps, get up from the table and cook your own food just the way you like it.

Become more proactive. Set standards and boundaries in your life. You can't tell a man that he's crossed the line if there wasn't one there in the first place. I've come to learn that we attract who we are. Often females with little to no boundaries attract males with no regard for those boundaries anyway. Here is a quick example of how clearly set boundaries can impact your life. Many years ago some major cities were built with walls around them for protection. In order to enter the city, otherwise known as the place of comfort, you had to submit yourself for inspection at a small entranceway leading into the city. The protective wall often spanned miles and miles around with only one small entryway. At the entryway you would find heavily armed guards monitoring all those attempting to enter the city. Those who were unauthorized or posed a threat to the quality of life behind the walls were denied entry. Those who added value to life behind the walls were admitted into the city.

The environment by the entryway was very tense and confrontational. It was a complete contrast from the flourishing atmosphere inside the city. Why such a positive atmosphere inside the city? It's because those inside the place of comfort were those who deserved to be there. This isn't meant to be a history lesson but rather an example of how to govern our own lives. We should have boundaries and walls that surround our lives. We ought to guard the entryway carefully, inspecting those who wish to gain access into our lives. **This is very important**. What took place outside the city walls had no effect on the quality of life inside the city. Your life should be the same way. And it can be. Imagine if all of the men in your life added to the quality of your life. Many of your lives are engulfed in constant turbulence as a result of the men you've allowed into your place of comfort. Some of you don't set any boundaries whatsoever in your life. Others of you put up walls and set boundaries, but you fail to properly inspect the men wishing to gain entry into your life. You allow in every male and wonder why the quality of your life is constantly diminishing. If your living room had white carpet, I'd be willing to bet most of you would make everyone who wished to come in your house take off his/her shoes first. If some of you would only learn to treat your life like your living room, your "carpet" would be a lot cleaner. You must tell yourself, "If it's going to happen, it's up to me."

Before you can pursue life's best, you must first realize that it's available. Second, before you can ever grasp it, you must believe that you deserve it. One of the goals of this book is to inspire you to go after life's best while empowering you to attain it. The choice is yours. You've read countless chapters, but now is when we find out whether or not it was worth your time. Will you be one to take action and make the proper adjustments in your life so you can see different results? Or will you revert to your "normal" way of living? Will YOU finally decide to change your life? Will you finally stop making excuses for your situation? You cannot make excuses and progress at the same time. Today you must choose one or the other. Continue to make excuses and stay where you are, or begin to make decisions that will brighten your future. It is my hope that if nothing else, all who are reading these pages at least recognize how powerful they are as women. I plead with you to come to grips with the fact that you have power over your own life, and over the men involved in it. One last time for good measure, when it comes to your life we men can only go as far as you let us, PERIOD.

Don't allow me to treat you any kind of way. Don't settle for me not being monogamous in our relationship. Don't give me your body without first proving that I'm worthy of such a gift. Please don't surrender your heart to me without being absolutely sure that I can be trusted with it. Refuse to let me in your life if I cannot add to the quality of it. Please stop sleeping with me on the first date. Make me respect you. Make me work. Make me sweat, and most of all, please make me be a man before you ever concede to becoming my woman. Live life. Love life and Give life, from my heart to yours.

Love,
Kevin Carr

"May GOD be your eternal source of strength, hope, and ability."

**If All Men Are Dogs, Then Women, You Hold the Leash:
How Far We Go Depends on You**

**By
Kevin Carr**

Breinigsville, PA USA
12 January 2011
253126BV00006B/17/P